I0039752

HUMMING-BIRDS.

HUMMING BIRDS

Peruvian Coquette & Crimson Topaz

HUMMING-BIRDS.

BY

Mary and Elizabeth Kirby,

AUTHORS OF "THINGS IN THE FOREST," ETC.

———— ◆ ————

LONDON:

T. NELSON AND SONS, PATERNOSTER ROW;

EDINBURGH; AND NEW YORK.

1874.

HUMMING – BIRDS

BY

MARY and ELIZABETH KIRBY

All rights reserved, which include the right to reproduce this book or portions thereof in any form except provided by U.S. Copyright Laws.

Digital Scanning and Publishing is a leader in the electronic republication of historical books and documents. We publish many of our titles as eBooks, paperback and hardcover editions. DSI is committed to bringing many traditional and well-known books back to life, retaining the look and feel of the original work.

Trade Paperback 10-digit ISBN: 1-58218-845-9
13-digit ISBN: 978- 1-58218-845-4

©2010 DSI Digital Reproduction
First DSI Printing: August 2010

Published by Digital Scanning Inc. Scituate, MA 02066
781-545-2100 http://www.Digitalscanning.com and
http://www.PDFLibrary.com

Contents.

HUMMING-BIRDS.

CHAPTER I

INTRODUCTORY.

THE Humming-Bird is a relation of the bird called the Sun-Bird, but is rather different in his habits. He hovers over flowers, and sucks the juices, without settling upon them. Poised in the air, he peeps cautiously, with his sparkling eye, into the recesses of the flower, vibrating his wings so rapidly that you can hardly see them. All the time, he makes a low humming sound, that is

very pleasant to listen to, and that seems
to lull the insects within the flower to sleep.
Then out darts his long delicate tongue,
and takes them up, one after the other;
and he finishes by sipping a little honey.

All the strength of the Humming-Bird
lies in his wings, that are large in propor-
tion to his tiny body. They are a little
like those of the Swift in shape; and
everybody knows how rapidly the Swift
can dart about, and cleave the air with his
pinions. The feathers on the quills of
the Humming-Bird's wing are so firmly
united that they are almost like a thin plate
of whalebone. No air can pass through
them, and this is why they make a humming sound, as the bird vibrates his wings.

The Humming-Bird needs these strong
wings to support himself in the air, as his
feet are too weak and delicate to perch for
any length of time.

And he depends very much upon his wings for safety.

There will come seasons of rain and storm, and his little nest will be beaten down, and his home among the trees and flowers be made a wreck. Before this happens, he must fly many long miles to get from beneath the clouds. He looks too fairy-like to undertake such a journey; but his wings are powerful enough to bear him out of reach of danger. They will transport him to other lands, where the storm has passed, and the trees and flowers are blooming as gaily as ever.

The long bill of the Humming-bird has been given him that he may search to the bottom of the large tubular flowers, and rifle their sweet juices. But some of these flowers are so bent that a straight bill would not be able to reach the honey; so the bird that feeds upon them has his bill

curved upwards at the tip, that he may
follow the bend of the flower, and not be
disappointed of his feast.

The tongue is not unlike the tongue of
the Woodpecker, and is darted out in the
same way, and for the same purpose—of
entrapping insects.

It is composed of two tubes, joined
together nearly the whole of their length,
and ending in a spoon-like point. It is
very sticky, so the insects when touched
by it cannot escape ; and it is also fringed
with minute spines or bristles, that still
further help to secure the prey.

The forest, with its great trees covered
with climbing-plants and flowers, swarms
with these brilliant little creatures.

> " Like fairy sprites, a thousand birds
> Glance by on golden wing ;
> Birds lovelier than the lovely hues
> Of the bloom wherein they sing."

No wonder the ancient Mexicans stole the

plumage of the Humming-Birds to adorn their mantles ; and very superb these mantles were, sparkling with many-coloured tints. And the Mexican youth thought he could make no more costly present to his bride than the gorgeous crest of the Humming-Bird, to be worn amongst her hair. Even now, the Indian women hang the tiny bodies of the Humming-Birds to their ears, instead of ear-rings ; and on their head-dresses, instead of jewels.

The Humming-Bird, though so small, is very brave, and will attack a bird three or four times his own size. It is no pleasant thing to come in the way of his long bill, for he always pecks at the eyes of his assailant.

When he is keeping watch over the nest, he is particularly fierce ; and if another bird happen to come near, he darts out, screaming with rage ; his throat swells, and his wings expand to their fullest extent, and he looks like a little fury.   He gives battle to the intruder, and the two birds fight desperately, until one of them falls to the ground exhausted, and so ends the conflict.

I am afraid the Humming-Bird is a very passionate little fellow.   He will even go into a rage with a flower that does not please him, or has not so much honey in it as he expected ; and then he tears it to pieces, and scatters it with his bill and claws.

Perhaps the best part of his character comes out when he is helping his little partner to build their nest.   He brings her all the materials, and flies about collecting them with the greatest industry. The tiny nest is generally hung to the end of a twig of the orange or pomegranate tree, and is completely hidden by one of the large leaves, that overhangs it, and forms a canopy. The nest is sometimes made entirely of thistle-down; and the prickly burs of the thistle are stuck outside to protect it. But moss and cotton are used quite as often, and dead leaves woven in among them.

The cotton grows upon a tree called the silk-cotton tree, that is a native of tropical countries. It is a very large tree indeed, and is looked upon by the black people with great veneration. They never venture to throw a stone at it; and when they are obliged to cut it down, they pour some wine at its root, in order to prevent it being angry, and doing them any harm! It is one of the few trees that shed their leaves; for a tropical forest is always green and full of foliage, as the new leaves come out before the old ones drop.

But, every other year, the silk-cotton

tree stands quite bare, and without a single leaf; and then its trunk and great branches are dotted all over with seed-pods.) As soon as the pods are ripe they burst, and out comes a quantity of fine silky down, that is carried away by the wind. It cannot be used as cotton, for it will not twist or hold together, and all that can be done with it is to stuff pillows and mattresses. But, as it floats hither and thither, it is a rich harvest for the little Humming-Birds. Hundreds of them may be seen darting about, pursuing the tufts of down, and carrying them away in their bills. When the nest is made, the mother bird lays two eggs in it, no bigger than peas, and of a snow-white colour, speckled here and there with yellow.

She and her mate sit upon the nest by turns, and never leave it a moment. At the end of twelve days the two little

Humming-Birds come out of their shells, and are about the size of blue-bottle flies. At first they are unfledged, but very soon are covered with down; and in time, feathers grow upon them, and become as beautiful as those of the parent birds.

CHAPTER II.

THE beautiful birds we are now describing are divided into families or groups.

There is one tribe of Humming-Birds that have their home in the shade of the forest. They obtain their food from leaves, since but few flowers are met with in these secluded and shady places. They search for insects on the vast tropical foliage of the trees, threading their way about with great dexterity, and picking off the insects that swarm above and beneath.

The Humming-Birds of the forest are

HUMMING BIRDS

The Sun Gem and the Brilliant

very numerous. Their nests are made of the fibres of plants, and dry mosses and lichens, closely woven together. They are often lined with the beautiful silk-cotton of which I have spoken, and that provides such abundant materials for the birds. The nest is long, and shaped like a purse. There is a Humming-Bird, in South America, that leads almost the life of a moth or a bat. It has two long tail-feathers that cross each other; and its dress is red and gold and green, and changes colour every moment.

It chooses the woods by the side of rivers, and dark and lonely places. Very early in the morning the bird comes out of its retreat in search of insects. But no sooner does the sun appear, and his flaming rays light up the sky, than the Humming-Bird disappears. It dislikes the glare and heat of the tropical day, and

2

hides in its cool retreat until the evening.
Then it comes out again, and darts hither
and thither in search of its prey.   But for
its brilliant colours, you might take it for
a bird of night.

The nest is built on a twig that overhangs some lonely creek.   It is very much
like a piece of tanned leather, and has a
kind of ridge or rim round the top.

This rim is to prevent the eggs from
rolling out.

The range of the Humming-Birds, like
that of the Parrots, is wider than was once
imagined.

The tropical region is their natural
home ; and every attempt to rear them in
our colder climate has been in vain.

But they have been known to wander
far beyond the limits of the Torrid Zone.
They pay flying visits to Canada, and
even travel as far as the land of the Seal

and the Penguin.   In the Southern
Hemisphere, Humming-Birds have been
seen in Patagonia.   But this seems to
have been a mere summer excursion, for
they retreated before the first breath of
autumn.

CHAPTER III.

THERE is a part of South America which is, next to Thibet, the highest country in the world. It is a kind of plateau situated between two ranges of the Andes, and is very much larger than England. Indeed, it would take nine such islands as England to make one tract of country like Bolivia.

I have brought you here, because in Bolivia, and also in Peru, there are some of the beautiful birds we are describing.

The Phaon Comet is a creature of rare and exquisite loveliness. Indeed, it flashes,

and sparkles, and glitters like one of those
glowing and wandering meteors above.

Nothing can be more gorgeous than its
attire. The feathers of the back are a
deep luminous crimson, its throat is like an
emerald, and the magnificent tail-feathers
are barred with black.

It has all the habits of its race, and
perhaps a larger share of courage and of
swiftness. It sweeps through the air with
whirling headlong movements. Sometimes the eye is wearied with these ceaseless evolutions, and then the bird will
drop, like a falling star, into some huge
blossom, and be hidden from sight.

In the high table-land of Bolivia the
cold is intense, and the icy wind sweeps
over with chilling breath. The soil is
barren and unfruitful; and we look in
vain for the birds and flowers of the
Tropics. But the deep sheltered valleys

are fertile in the extreme, and produce sugar, cotton, and all the riches of a sunny clime.

The table-land, cold and rugged as it is, has many inhabitants; for here are found those wonderful mines of gold and silver that were such a source of wealth to the Spaniards. And here a city was built, called Potosi, which is the most elevated city in the world.

The mountain on which the city stands is pierced in every direction by the shafts of mines. At night, when the mines were working, and used to glow with the light of innumerable furnaces, the sight was very grand indeed.

At one time, more than fifteen thousand persons were employed at the mines. But the veins of ore are now less productive, and are comparatively deserted.

You may imagine the desolate state of

the country round Potosi; nothing is to be seen but bare rocks, covered with moss. The mountains are tipped with perpetual snow.

The poor Indian would fare badly enough, but for certain plants, which are given by Nature for his comfort. There is a plant which grows at a great height above the sea, and in places where no other seed or grain could ripen. It is called *quinoa*, and the seeds can be prepared in many different ways. The leaves can also be made into a kind of beer.

But the greatest consolation to the Indian is another plant called *coca*, which is abundant in the sheltered valleys. It thrives in these tropical spots, and also on the heights, and is as carefully cultivated and as important as the crop of corn is with us.

The plantations of coca are seen on the

steep sides of the valleys, rising to an amazing height above the level of the sea. The plant is about the size of our English blackthorn, and has a shining green foliage and small white flowers, which ripen into scarlet berries.

The berries are not used, but the leaves are gathered and dried in the sun. They are chewed by the Indian with great delight; and he is never seen without his leathern pouch full of coca, and which also contains a little box of powdered lime.

His manner of chewing is to work up the morsel of coca into a ball, then, taking it from his mouth, he plunges a piece of wood like a tooth-pick into the lime, and pierces the ball through and through with it until it gets the taste of lime. That is just how he likes it.

But one ball will not content him, and he goes on chewing until he is often in a

HUMMING BIRDS

Bison Comet & Hill Star

state of intoxication. Thus a valuable plant is made a source of evil. But the Indian would not give up his coca on any terms whatever ; he stops his work three times a day in order to chew it, and it serves him almost in the stead of food.

CHAPTER IV.

ONE of the luxuriant valleys situated among the Andes is called the Valley of Quito. Here is the capital city of a portion of South America named Quito, a province that includes hill and dale, rock and mountain, and all kinds of temperatures and productions. The climate of the valley is delicious. Here seems to reign an ever verdant spring. No extremes of heat or cold reach this favoured spot.

It is clothed with fruitful fields and orchards, and flocks and herds, and populous villages. It looks to the traveller the abode of beauty and content. But the most dangerous volcanoes in the world hem in the lovely valley of Quito.

Smoke and flame are often seen issuing from their snow-clad tops. The snow will suddenly melt before some violent eruption, and floods will desolate the happy valley.

The flames of Cotopaxi, the most famous of the volcanoes, have been known to rise three thousand feet above the top of the mountain, and its frightful roar is heard a hundred and fifty miles distant !

Nothing can be more dangerous than the neighbourhood of these volcanoes. Under ground are stores of hidden fire, and elements of mischief that break out with violence.

The inhabitants are always in danger of earthquakes. Then the scene baffles

description.   The earth reels and groans,
trees are torn up by the roots, and rocks
are rent · into fragments.   Blue flames
issue from the ground, and people and
houses, flocks and herds, are involved in
destruction.

The natives of Quito may be said to
live in perpetual hazard.   But they do
not seem to realize the fact.   They are a
gay, light-hearted race, fond of pleasure,
and of revelling in all the delights of
their beautiful country.   For here, as if
to atone for other drawbacks, the fruits
of the earth ripen with wonderful rapid-
ity.   Sowing and reaping are carried on
at once.

There is a mighty peak of the Andes,
said by some to be the highest peak in
the world.   It is not a volcano, but its
sides are thickly covered with snow; and
though in the midst of the Tropics, the

temperature in the neighbourhood is intensely cold.

Yet I have brought you here to behold the spot where a Humming-Bird chooses to dwell! He has his name from the mountain, and is called the Chimborazian Hill-Star.

A star of beauty indeed he is! His costume is magnificent. The head and throat are violet, and there is a ring of shining green round the neck. The white of the under part of his body contrasts with the brilliant colours that adorn him. His bill is black as jet.

This star-like creature haunts the grand mountain of Chimborazo, and ascends nearly to the line where snow commences.

Here grows the gray lichen, the last of the plants, lingering on the verge of eternal snow. Lower down are stunted bushes and meadows of saxifrage ; and

then comes the wax-palm, its leaves
coated with a substance like wax.

Lower still is the grotesque orchis, the
pine-apple, the fern, the laurel, and the
fragrant myrtle.

As you descend, the colours deepen in
richness, and the climate becomes more
and more tropical, until, at length, you
find yourself among the rich foliage and
gorgeous flowers of the Torrid Zone.
Thus a succession of pictures are pre-
sented by the hand of Nature.

The Humming-Bird feeds on the Alpine plants, and makes his nest of moss
and lichen, and fastens it under the ledge
of a rock. Here the mother bird lays two
tiny eggs, from which the young Humming-Birds will issue.

CHAPTER V.

IN the early spring, when the warm sun brings out countless flowers and blossoms, the inhabitants of the United States, and other portions of North America, are rejoiced to behold a fairy creature, light as air, and with resplendent colours, advance to the gardens and groves. Its gorgeous throat glows with fiery red; the feathers are very strong, and lie upon each other like scales. As the bird moves they change from crimson to black, and from black to crimson.

Its costume of lustrous green changes
and sparkles like the light of emeralds.
Its movements are as the lightning-flash,
or the glow of a sunbeam.   It darts
from flower to flower like a gleam of
light, visiting orchard and prairie and
grove.

The whole land, with its mighty forests,
vast meadows, and majestic rivers, is as
one garden of delight.   The bird is recog-
nized and admired everywhere.

"The Ruby-throated Humming-Bird
is come!"

Many a long stretch of country, over
hill, dale, river, and forest, have the wings
of the bird borne it in safety.   It is provided with no weapons of defence.   It
owes its safety to its rapid flight, its courage, and its minute size, which screens it
from observation.

Now it appears in full beauty, and prepared to sport through the long summer hours with ever new delight!

It has its favourites amongst the flowers. Do you see that brilliant sheet of scarlet ? That is the trumpet-flower, which the Humming-Bird loves.

It comes to the blossom, and poises over it a few seconds. Its wings are like a mist, and are almost invisible as they vibrate in the air. But you can catch sight of the ruby throat, and the golden-green of the back.

Presently the bill is thrust into the flower, and picks out an insect. Then the bird retires to some withered twig, on which it perches to arrange its plumage. Its note is like the chirp of the grasshopper, and is now and then uttered as it flits from flower to flower, or when it is engaged in battle with one of its companions.

The Humming-Bird is very brave.   It will attack a bird double its own size; even the tyrant Fly-catcher is often driven away, and pursued for a short distance.

Now and then the great humble-bee comes droning by, and makes an attack on the radiant creature in its path.   But there is little danger from such a clumsy foe.   The Humming-Bird darts away, and is out of sight in a moment.

Its own flight is like that of the bee, only far more rapid.   It darts in at the open window of a room, attracted by the scent of some fragrant bouquet.   It gives the flowers a passing notice, and is gone ere you can well behold it.

When the season grows late, and the evenings are cool, the Humming-Bird can find many places of refuge.

It enters the hothouse or conservatory, and uses it for a sleeping-room ; going thence in the morning, and returning at night.   When the season gets later still, the Humming-Bird disappears altogether.

Cold is very dreadful to this child of the Tropics.   Sun and heat are necessary to its existence.   If deprived of them it dies.

A Humming-Bird was once put into a cage, and placed in a shady room.   The weather was cool, and the poor little bird, after fluttering about for a time, fell down as if stupified.   It lay with its eyes closed, and giving no signs of life.   The owner of the bird carried it out of doors, and placed it in the sun.

Quickly a change was observed.   The bird began to breathe more freely ; its eyes opened, and even sparkled with their usual brilliancy.

When it had quite recovered, no further effort was made to detain it, and it flew joyfully to the top of a tree, and, perching on a branch, began to dress its plumage.

The rays of the sun had restored the bird to life.

The nest of the Ruby-throated Humming-Bird is the most delicate fabric that ever was seen. The outside is made of the same gray old lichen that coats over the branch where the tiny nest is fixed. The bird works with such skill that it contrives to make the nest look as if it were part of the branch. The atoms of lichen that it uses are gummed together with saliva. The next coating is of some silky down it has picked up; and the innermost lining of all is of the softest fibres of plants, that make a silken couch for the eggs to lie upon.

CHAPTER VI.

THE HUMMING-BIRD OF NOOTKA SOUND.

ON the western coast of North America, as far north as the Temperate Zone, is a bay, or, as it is called, a *sound*. The entrance lies between two rocky points, and when these are cleared, the bay widens out and contains a number of islands of different extent.

Many years ago, Captain Cook entered this sound, and was the first to discover its existence. He anchored his ship near to one of the larger islands, and gave the bay the name of Nootka Sound, which it has retained ever since.

The climate here is very mild,—much milder than on the opposite coast of America, in precisely the same latitude.

Here were woods of the lime and cypress, and other trees; and though the gorgeous flowers we have spoken of were not to be seen, yet others of a humbler form and colour sprinkled the earth. Strawberries, raspberries, and currants grew in abundance; and the buttercup, the wild-rose, and many of our English weeds, were in full bloom.

Squirrels were at play among the branches of the trees; and there were a few species of birds, such as Eagles, Woodpeckers, Kingfishers; and on the coast there were Swans, and Gulls, and Wild-Ducks.

But a discovery was made in this sequestered spot by Captain Cook. He saw one of the beautiful birds of which we are speaking. It is called the Ruff-necked Humming-Bird, or the " Humming-Bird of Nootka Sound."

In one of his excursions on the island, he came upon a number of brilliant birds, glowing with the rich colours of their tribe, and flashing from flower to flower, or poising over them with the habit peculiar to their race.

As he approached a bush, out darted a radiant creature, like a flame of fire, and passed close by him, as though it would attack his face, returning again and again to the charge, and whirling about in the utmost fury.

This was the male bird, on the watch to drive away any intruder from the nest. The angry, hissing noise it made, was like that of a ball as it whizzes through the air.

A few days after, Captain Cook found

the nest on the forked branch of a bramble. The mother bird was sitting on her eggs. She flew out, and hovered near him while he examined the nest. But when he went away, she took her place again, and continued to sit on her eggs as before. The nest was as tiny and light as possible. It was made of lichen and moss, and a few feathers woven together with the slender rootlets of plants, and was lined with thistle-down.

The plumage of the bird is soft and beautifully blended, and glossed like velvet. The upper parts are a rich orange, and the head a bronzed green and purple. The feathers of the throat and the sides of the neck are a magnificent fiery red, with a tint of yellow or green, according to the light in which you see them. On the lower part of the neck is a band of reddish-white.

On a clear day, the bird may be seen rising high in the air, and then descending, to mount again. While it descends, it utters a curious note, which resembles the noise made by the branches of a tree as they rub together in a high wind.

This singular note would hardly be supposed to proceed from a bird, still less from the tiny creature that produces it. If the weather is dull or cloudy, the Humming-Bird is silent.

The mother bird wears a different costume to that of her mate. She is clad in golden-green; and instead of the orange throat, she has spots of a glowing ruby.

In this remote and inhospitable spot, where we should least expect to find them, do we thus come upon the beautiful birds!

CHAPTER VII.

THE MANGO HUMMING-BIRD.

THERE is one species of Humming-Bird that is more hardy than the rest of its tribe, and has been brought to England.

It is called the Mango Humming-Bird, and is very common in the parts of the world where it lives. The Mango Humming-Birds are seen everywhere.

They are beautiful birds, as you will judge from the description I am about to give you.

Under the throat and body is a deep rich stripe of velvety black, shaded with the brilliant blue which so often makes part of the costume of the Humming-Bird.

The upper part of the body is the usual golden-green. The tail-feathers are rounded at the tip, and are violet or purple, according to the light in which you see them.

A female Humming-Bird was once sitting in her nest, when a young man who was passing saw her. He contrived to cut off the branch with the nest and the bird together, and to bring them away. A few days after, he sailed for England, and during the passage he fed the bird with honey and water. She grew very tame, and continued to hatch her eggs, out of which came, in course of time, two tiny creatures no bigger than blue-bottle flies.

These little Humming-Birds began to

grow and thrive. But the mother did not long survive her imprisonment. She very soon died, and the young birds were left to the care of their owner.

He contrived to keep them alive for some few weeks after they reached England, in spite of the coolness of the climate. One of the tiny gems was petted by a lady, who allowed it to sip honey from her lips.

The home of the Mango Humming-Bird is in the West Indies, and in the flowery land of Florida.

Parts of this beautiful country abound with flowers; so much so, that its name has been given to it on this very account. Orange and lemon trees grow wild in the utmost abundance, and their blossoms afford a delicious banquet to the birds. Cotton is produced in great plenty in this tropical clime; and the rich dye called indigo is brought from here.

The indigo-plant is a child of the sun, and cannot thrive anywhere but in the Tropics. Indeed, it requires a certain temperature to enable it to vegetate.

It is a shrub-like plant, rising about two feet from the ground, and its leaves a little resemble those of the acacia. When it begins to flower, the owner of the plantation cuts it down with a sickle; and then it will sprout again, and bear a second crop. In this genial clime, the planter will sometimes obtain four crops a year.

In the mighty forests of this part of the world, where the trunks and branches of the trees are clothed with brilliant parasites and spikes of flowers of every hue, the Humming-Birds are met with by thousands.

And in the gardens and cultivated places they are equally abundant; and so devoid of fear, that a bird will hover over a blossom while the owner is plucking another from the same bush!

The mango itself is one of the beneficent trees of the Tropics. It has great spreading branches; and the foliage is so dense that a fugitive may hide amidst it, and be rarely found by his pursuers, though they are searching the very tree.

The taste of the fruit is sweet and luscious, and in the season the black people live almost entirely upon it. The cattle also are fed, and even fattened, upon mangoes. In Jamaica, a basket of mangoes may be had for the trouble of climbing the tree and shaking the branches.

HUMMING BIRDS

Coras Shear Tail and Purple Crest

CHAPTER VIII.

THERE is a naturalist who has spent much time and labour in studying the habits of the Humming-Bird. He has given us a great deal of information about them, in a book written for the purpose, and which is the most valuable we have on the subject.

There is a lovely bird named after him, "Gould's Humming-Bird," or "Gould's Coquette."

It is one of the most beautiful of its tribe. Its head and crest are of vivid red; its wings are purple; and it wears on its

neck a frill of long white feathers tipped
with golden-green.

There is a strong likeness said to exist
between the Humming-Birds and some of
the insect tribe. The Humming-Bird
seems more allied to the moth or the
butterfly than to the rest of the birds.
There is one moth so much like it, that
the naturalist has been known to shoot it
by mistake for the tiny gem we have been
describing. It is called the "humming-
bird hawk-moth." It is rather smaller
than the Humming-Bird, but has just the
same habits. It darts and whirls about
with wonderful quickness, and hovers over
the flower just as the bird does.

It has a long trunk or proboscis, which
it thrusts into the flower in search of food.
At the end of its body is a tuft or brush,
which, when spread open, is not unlike the
tail of a bird.

The natives of Brazil seem much struck with the likeness we are speaking of. They believe that the moth turns into the bird, and that the bird was first a moth. They tried to impress their fancy on a naturalist who was visiting that part of the world.

" Look," they said to him ; " their heads are the same, and so are their tails."

The naturalist found it impossible to argue them out of this belief.

Even an English gentleman once stoutly maintained that he had seen a Humming-Bird in England.   For one species of the hawk-moth is found in our own country ; and you may see it whirling and hovering and darting about in our gardens.   The gentleman had seen the moth, and had mistaken it for a Humming-Bird.

The orange-groves, in those sunny lands where the Humming-Birds live, are covered all the year round with blossom. But at certain seasons their beauty reaches perfection. They are a mass of fruit and blossom.

Then come the beautiful birds in flocks, sparkling and shining and glistening in the sun like gold and gems.

They whirl about the trees, darting so swiftly that you can scarcely see them. When they pause, it is but for a moment. Down goes the bill, and the bird is off again, darting from blossom to blossom, not in a regular manner, but at random, and as by caprice.

Sometimes two Humming-Birds come to the same flower. Then they quarrel violently, and mount upwards, doing fierce battle with each other. But the storm soon passes over, and the birds dart off again in search of insects. Their movements are so rapid that the eye cannot catch the brilliant colours that adorn them. Nor can one species be distinguished from another, unless there happens to be a conspicuous patch of white mixed with the lovely tints of their plumage.

I should tell you that the female Humming-Bird does not wear the brilliant colours of her mate. She is dressed in a more sober costume, and is therefore not so much prized.

CHAPTER IX.

THE MARVELLOUS HUMMING-BIRD.

THE Marvellous Humming-Bird has perhaps no equal in beauty in the world. It is a creature that floats about on wings of azure and emerald. It wears a crown of brilliant blue, and a collar of green encircles the throat. The sides of the breast are a soft white; and the wonderful tail-feathers—that project to a great length—are tipped with brown.

This rare creature was first discovered in Peru,—a country of both desert and of verdure, of rich tropical spots and of burning sand.

This curious region, which presents such different aspects, lies on the sea-coast, between the great mountains of the Cordilleras and the Pacific Ocean.

Rain seldom falls here, and the green spots are caused by some rill or stream that descends from the mountains. The inhabitants prize every drop of the precious stream, and use it to water their fields and gardens. At the line where the artificial system of irrigation ends, the desert again begins.

On these spots, thus won from the sand, all the rich verdure of the Tropics is seen. Here is cotton, and sugar, and maize, and the products of a burning clime. And here are beautiful birds of every shade and hue. Here is the Parrot, and the Pigeon, and the Crowned Fly-catcher, dressed in a costume of fiery red.

In this strange land, mist supplies the

place of rain. At a certain season of the year there comes a veil over the sky, and a kind of ceaseless drizzle takes place.

The drizzle, unpleasant as it must be, falls on the barren places and dry arid plains with all the blessing of dew or of rain. They become green and fertile, and the whole land rejoices.

Myriads of sea-birds are found on the shore; and on some islands close by, successive generations have made their home for centuries.

As no rain falls, the droppings of the birds have been accumulating for ages, and would remain undisturbed, if man had not found out their value. His ships go constantly to fetch away the bird-manure, or guano, as it is called. It is of the greatest benefit to the farmer, and used by him to enrich his land. Not a mine of gold or silver could be more important.

CHAPTER X.

THE HUMMING-BIRD OF ROBINSON CRUSOE'S ISLAND.

SOME long time ago, a Spanish sailor used to steer his vessel backwards and forwards between Peru and Chili.

He was always baffled by contrary winds, and it occurred to him that if he stood out farther to sea he might escape them.

He put this idea in practice; and during his next voyage, when at sea, he fell in with an island hitherto undiscovered. From a distance, the island looked like a mass of rocks and mountains, and had a barren appearance. But as he approached, the prospect improved : the mountains were clothed with trees ; and there were fertile valleys, watered by crystal streams. And here and there a cascade bounded from rock to rock, and glided along like a thread of silver.

All kinds of tropical plants and trees grew on the sheltered parts of the island. Here were palm-trees, and the cotton, and the pepper ; and here were myrtle-trees of great size, so that the trunks could be sawed into planks forty feet long.

A tall grass, as high as a man, covered these fertile spots, and looked like a crop of oats. And there were ferns, and creepers, and clover, and many other familiar plants. The island had no human inhabitants ; but birds and insects were met with. Here were great spiders, that wove gigantic webs from tree to tree. And

here were the Albatross and the Hawk;
and a bird that made a hole in the ground,
like a rabbit, and fed upon fish. Every
night, this bird used to utter a note like
the words " Be quiet !"

And here were Humming-Birds in all
their brilliant beauty. Perhaps the most
beautiful Humming - Bird ever seen is
found in this remote spot. It was discovered, not many years ago, by Captain
King, and its name added to the list of
Humming-Birds that were known to live
in the island.

The blue crown of the bird is composed
of scaly feathers, which spread out to some
length, and form a crest of surpassing
beauty.

The upper part of the body is a bright
emerald-green, and the two middle feathers
of the tail are green; the others, green
outside and a clear white beneath. The

cheeks of this wonderful bird are a purple-green, with pink or violet spots, according to the light. The under part of the body is pure white, with round spots of the richest golden-green, that contrast with the snowy ground on which they are marked.

Nothing can exceed the splendour of this magnificent bird. Indeed, every description falls short of the reality. It is as if Nature in this remote spot excelled herself. The name by which the brilliant gem is known is "Stokes's Humming-Bird."

The Spanish sailor gave his own name to the island, and called it Juan Fernandez. He was allowed to possess the newly-discovered spot, and even made an attempt to colonize it. But the few families who went to settle there did not remain. They soon abandoned it, and it was uninhabited as before.

Juan Fernandez is known to every reader of " Robinson Crusoe," as the island on which he and his man Friday lived in solitude.

The real solitary, or exile, was a seaman of the name of Alexander Selkirk, who quitted his vessel, and was left behind in this desolate place. He spent four years without hearing the sound of a human voice, and was at last picked up and brought to England. The goats, in whose skins he had clothed himself, were the descendants of those animals brought by the colonists I have mentioned, and that had multiplied and overrun the island.

CHAPTER XI.

THE AZURE CROWN HUMMING-BIRD.

IN the tropical regions of Brazil, the birds have no need to migrate, from one part of the country to another, to escape the winter. There is no cold season to drive them from their haunts and homes. So that the Cuckoo never flits, as she does in England, and the Swallow is seen making his aërial curves and sweeps the whole year round.

But many reasons impel the birds at times to wander.

At one season of the year, great rains

HUMMING BIRDS
Golden Tail and the Azure Crown

fall and deluge the ground. Then, the forest becomes too damp and cool to be pleasant to the birds.

And more than that — in the open country an abundant banquet is awaiting them. The trees are loaded with the most tempting fruit. Here are ripe oranges, hanging in profusion, their golden hue displaying itself amid the flowers and blossoms of the tree.

Here is the banana, and many more, bending under their rich burden. The maize-fields and the rice-fields are equally tempting ; and such a lure cannot be resisted.

Forth come the birds, from the damp gloomy forest, to the fields, and groves, and uplands.

Each bird makes for its especial food. The Parrots fall upon the fields of maize ; the Toucans devour the bananas with keen

relish; and the Finch tribe, clad in costume of blue and scarlet, make for the
rice.

Many beautiful birds, rarely seen at
other times, are now abroad, flaunting
their rich plumage in the open fields.

The Indian hunter, and the white man
who has settled in the country, takes, the
one his rifle, and the other his blow-pipe
and his poisoned arrow.

The white man can shoot numbers of
beautiful birds without much trouble. The
gay Cotinga, the Parrot, and the Toucan,
fall alike beneath his gun.

The Indian is on the watch for a splendid Macaw, that is generally out of his
reach in the recesses of the forest.

But the magnificent bird, with its flaming colours, has ventured from its retreat,
to banquet on certain fruits in which it
delights, and which grow in the open

country. The Indian shoots as many Macaws as he can. He has an eye for colour, and he uses their feathers to plume his arrows, and to adorn his person.

In these bird-hunting expeditions, the Indian is more patient and hardy than the white man. He continues his watch for days with the utmost vigilance; and his quick ear and eye can detect sounds and signals, when his more civilized neighbour would be at fault.

This rich and varied country has its share of Humming-Birds.

Among the beautiful birds that shine and glisten, they take their place. The perpetual summer, the gorgeous flowers, the abundance of insects, render bird-life a continual banquet.

The Golden-green Humming-Bird is met with here, and is one of the smallest but most exquisite of the tribe.

The tiny creature wears, as its name indicates, a costume of golden-green with an ever-changing lustre. The. wings are a brownish-purple, and the tail an indigo-blue.

Then there is the bird which is called the Azure Crown—a bird of rare and enchanting beauty.

It is larger than the tiny gem just mentioned. The bill is a clear yellow with a black tip, and the under parts of the body a pure white.

On the back of the head is a hood or cowl of glittering blue, which is the " azure crown."

CHAPTER XII.

GOLDEN TAIL.

THE beautiful birds that abound in Brazil, as in all tropical countries, furnish a rich material for the native toilet—such a material as we in these colder climes cannot boast of. The ancient tribes of the country adorned themselves with the plumage of the birds, and nowhere could they obtain more rich variety. The Macaw, the Trogon, the Cotinga—almost all the birds we have named—yield plumes and feathers of wondrous beauty.

And the feather-flowers, made by the

Indians, are esteemed the loveliest ornaments by people of civilized countries, and
have made their way to Europe.

Now and then, a splendid bouquet is
purchased by the European, that is not
altogether what it professes. The leaves
should be made of the feathers of the
Parrot; but instead of this, the Indian
has procured plumes from the back
of some other bird more easily met
with—such as the white Ibis—and dyed
them to imitate the gaudy tints of the
Parrot.

The Scarlet Ibis and the Rose-coloured
Spoon-bill, both of which are found on
the shores of the mighty rivers that run
through the forest, yield the most gay-
coloured feathers.

The carnation, or the tulip, or even the
queen of the flowers, the rose, is imitated
with the most exquisite skill, and makes

an ornament of rare beauty for the tresses
of an Indian belle.

There is a certain tribe of Indians, living
on the banks of one of the rivers, that wear
a head-dress of the most gorgeous colours.

It is a coronet of red and yellow feathers, firmly plaited together, and fitted
to a fillet or band, encircling the head.
These feathers are not of their natural
colour. They belong to some of the trans-
formed Parrots of which I have spoken,
and are very highly prized. Nothing but
actual necessity will induce an Indian to
part with his head-dress.

The ladies of Brazil imitate this fashion
of wearing the feathers of birds. They
love to adorn themselves with flowers,
made of the bright-coloured plumage that
so delights the Indian.

And not one of the flowers, thus arti-
ficially produced, can vie with those made

from the breasts and the throats of the Humming-Birds. These exquisite ornaments can hardly be described. In the bonnet, or amid the hair, they flash and sparkle with wonderful brilliance. The emerald, the topaz, all the famous jewels of the East, seem to pale before them.

One of these gems of Nature, that inhabits the forests of Brazil, is called the "Golden Tail," and dazzles the eye with the swiftness of its movements.

The Golden Tail Humming-Bird wears a crown of rich dark blue, with a tinge of green. Green and gold adorn the upper surface of the body, and a golden tint flashes with remarkable brilliance from the under parts of the wings. The tail glistens with the richest tint of gold, and the under surface of the body is a shining green.

This rare creature flits and flashes in

the deep forests and open plains, in the gardens and the groves of Brazil.

But, besides the beautiful birds, the Indian has still another resource for his toilet. The insects, in this land of radiant colours, are in their way as splendid as the birds.

They shine and sparkle like living gold. The Indian will often make his flowers of the lustrous wings of a beetle ; or, treating the insect as if it were a precious stone, will have its body set in gold, like a brooch. And, as if Nature delighted in every form of radiance, and to flash and sparkle with increasing lustre before the eye, here are the whole race of fireflies, gleaming in the darkness like so many stars.

The Indian is attracted to them as to the beautiful birds. He captures the living spark, as it glows with its own light, and uses it for a torch to guide him through the forest gloom.

And the ladies place the brilliant spark amid their hair, letting it gleam and sparkle like a diamond; or they wear a robe of gossamer texture, through which glow a myriad of fire-flies, so that the wearer seems as if clad in a starry vesture!

CHAPTER XIII.

I HAVE not told you half the varieties met with in the costume of these beautiful birds.

There is an ornament worn by a Humming-Bird that lives in the forests of Brazil. This bird has two thick tufts of deep indigo-blue springing from under the eyes and forming a kind of ruff. Each tuft is tipped with yellow, which contrasts with the intense blue of the breast. On the forehead the feathers look like scales, and are of a bright green; and there is a band of deep velvety black running in a

line from eye to eye.   The throat and part
of the neck are of a shining green, and
here are long narrow feathers that form a
collar or breastplate of green against the
blue.

The tail-feathers are broad and ex-
panded, and of a metallic green.   It is
difficult to imagine such a rare and sump-
tuous creature, even in this land of
beauty.

There is a Humming-Bird also in Brazil
called the Tufted-neck Humming-Bird.
It wears a large crest of clear chestnut,
and the sides of the neck are adorned with
tufts of narrow feathers.   The tufts or
plumes are of the same colour as the crest,
and end in a tip of shining green.   The
throat and the upper part of the breast,
and also the forehead, are covered with
scale-like feathers of a brilliant green.
The back is of a bronzed green shaded

with blue, and separated from the tail-feathers by a band or stripe of white.

The tail is broad, and spreads out in a fan-like shape, and is green and chestnut, with shades of purple.

These exquisite little birds with the tufts and ruffs I have just described, are called by the French "Coquettes." This is a playful idea suggested by the ornament worn by the bird. It can set up its beautiful ruff, and give itself the most attractive appearance.

For it is during the courting season that the ruff appears in its full beauty.

Thousands of Humming-Birds, rare to us, but common enough in these sunny lands, sport in the forests of Brazil, and are clad in rainbow vesture.

The traveller beholds them as in a vast aviary, flashing brightness and beauty on every side.

Here are a whole bevy of beautiful birds. Crowds of Parrots sidle about on the branches, or dress their gaudy plumage; and here are the caressing Love-Birds, and the flaming Macaws; and close by sits the solemn Trogon in his resplendent plumes; and little gleams of blue and scarlet among the branches show the presence of innumerable Cotingas, as brisk and gay as possible.

Beneath, on the moist earth, are numbers of living creatures. Here are lizards, and snakes, and insects of every kind. Here is the armadillo, that rustles among the decaying leaves; and the curious ant-eater, with its long tongue and its clog-like feet; and a deer will now and then bound through some leafy opening, pursued by the jaguar; and the tapir, with its swine-like snout, will come crashing by.

Up above, in the topmost tier of branches, where giant trees push their crowns into light and air, is a vast leafy region, all matted and bound together by the ropes and cables of the forest.

On this mighty plateau the monkeys live in security, and run nimbly about, and grin and chatter and frolic. Not even the thunder and lightning of the white man's gun can reach them. And the squirrel bounds from bough to bough with wild delight.

Standing as we do in this magical spot, surrounded with all the wonders of the Tropics, a peculiar sound meets our ear.

There comes up from the distance a clear shrill whistle, like the well-known signal of a railway-train. Such a thing cannot be in this remote spot; but as sure as morning, noon, and evening come, it is heard.

A grasshopper makes this curious utterance—not more curious than another sound, like a hammer, that marks the hours through the tropical night with the utmost regularity.

This watchman of the night is a frog, called by the natives the "Hammer-smith."

And in the scorching noon, weary and parched with thirst, the traveller is sometimes mocked by a small brown bird that repeats in his ears the tantalizing words that mean, in the language of the country, "Have you no water?"

CHAPTER XIV.

THE CRIMSON TOPAZ.

THE part of the world in which the lovely bird called the Crimson Topaz is found, is rich in many interesting scenes and valuable productions.

It is called Guiana, and is a territory to the north of South America.

Here again the tropical forest presents every variety of wonder. The most curious object met with in its wild recesses is a tree called the mora, which towers aloft, its topmost branches often white and bare with age. A fig-tree that has the habits of a parasite chooses the mora to subsist upon.

The fig-tree is about the size of our English apple-tree, and it shoots forth from one of the thick branches of the mora near to the top.

When the figs are ripe, they yield a rich harvest to the birds. Crowds of birds flock round them, and to this very circumstance the fig-tree owed its existence.

A bird dropped the seed of the fig-tree on the branch of the mora. It had been feasting on some neighbouring figs, and had perched on the mora to digest its banquet.

Up to this time the mora was flourishing in all its luxuriance; but the seed dropped by the bird sent out its rootlets into the branches, and began to draw nourishment from the sap.

The sap caused it to grow with vigour

and mount upwards; but when it became a fig-tree yielding fruit, it also, though a parasite, became the abode of other parasites. The birds, as they flocked to it, dropped seeds that began to grow upon its branches, as its own seed had grown upon the mora-tree. Thus parasite after parasite took hold on each other, and all were maintained by the sap and juices of the mora!

But the tree, thus encumbered, cannot long support its burdens. After a time it will languish and decay. And then the whole brood of parasites, cut off from their supplies, will perish with it. Often, in the forest, the traveller stands to gaze on a tree so covered with parasites that not a vestige of the trunk or the branches can be seen.

Some of these parasites bear flowers of brilliant beauty, that seem to start, as by magic, from the branch or stem on which they grow.

And others have a strange and almost mournful aspect, as they hang from the tree like ragged tufts of hair.

They are known by the name of the " Monkey's Beard," or the " Old Man's Beard."

The thick black filaments of the plant are like horse-hair, and are used by the natives as such, to stuff their cushions and mattresses.

The birds find in this curious parasite a material ever at hand of which they can build their nests.

There is a little bird dressed in black and orange, and that is called the Baltimore. It picks up a long thread of the " beard," and fixes it by either end to a branch. This is the beginning of the nest. Then comes the other bird with another thread, and fixes it side by side with the first.

Thus the two birds assist each other in building the nest, and it is woven so firmly that no tempest and no rain can injure it.

The nest of the Crimson Topaz is made of a fungus, and fastened together with a fine net like a cobweb. It is of the shape of a cup, and is found in some sheltered spot, or dark and lonely creek.

The bird itself sparkles like a jewel, and well deserves its name of Topaz. Its colours are gorgeous, and the feathers seem to overlap each other like scales.

Nothing can be more splendid than the tail-feathers of this beautiful bird. They are orange and green, and the throat is the loveliest green and yellow.

The Crimson Topaz is the largest of the Humming-Birds. The mother bird lays two eggs in her cup-like nest.

CHAPTER XV.

THE PURPLE-CRESTED HUMMING-BIRD.

THE territory of Guiana abounds in many kinds of Humming-Birds. There is the Black-crested Humming-Bird, with a breastplate of emerald-green, while the centre of the breast is black; and the White-tailed Humming-Bird, with a tail of white, except the middle feathers, which are green.

And there is the Purple-crested Humming-Bird, with the upper part of the body a purplish-black, and the wings of an olive-green. The bright grass-green of the tail is very striking. This beautiful bird is to be seen in the West Indian Islands, as well as in Guiana.

The forests of Guiana swarm with birds of every hue and tint. Crowds of little creatures, some of them no bigger than a Wren, but clad in brilliant colours, fly about in troops, to seek for insects on the leaves and branches of the trees. These are the Manakins. They have a low sweet note, uttered from time to time as they hop about.

Then there is a bird like the Mocking-Bird, dressed in black and yellow, that makes all kinds of curious noises. Whatever bird happens to be singing, it will mimic him, and sing almost as well, so that there appears to be a succession of birds. Now you hear the cry of the Toucan, now the hammering of the Woodpecker. If even a dog bark, the sound will be mimicked!

In the most secluded part of the forest, a bird lives that is so rare that he is scarcely ever seen.

He is called the " Cock of the Rock," and wears a very beautiful costume of orange, and has on his head a great comb or crest that gives him his name.   These birds are said by the Indians to hold " dancing-parties," after the manner of the Birds of Paradise ; but in this case only one bird performs, and the rest look on and clap their wings by way of applause.

This is the moment chosen by the Indian to creep cautiously to the spot with his blow-pipe.

The birds are so occupied that they do not perceive his approach, until he has shot several of them.

CHAPTER XVI.

CORA SHEAR-TAIL HUMMING-BIRD.

EVERY part of the strange country of Peru is hilly, if not mountainous. The valleys are little better than ravines; and the rivers flow with the rushing noise of torrents, and fall in cascades of foam as they make their way to the sea.

A journey in Peru is attended with some difficulty. Along the desert strip of land near to the shore, heat, thirst, and fatigue, to say nothing of the attacks of robbers, are to be feared. But the interior of the country is beset

with many dangers and trials worse than
these.

Here are precipices of a frightful description, and glaciers, and avalanches;
and, indeed, all the risks and perils of an
Alpine country.

Sometimes the valley traversed is barely
wide enough to allow the travellers to
pass. It might be called a narrow cleft
between two perpendicular rocks, that
here and there nearly touch each other.

Masses of half-loosened rock threaten
to fall from the sides of the precipice every
moment. Nay, such a thing often takes
place, and mules, and even travellers, will
be swept into the abyss.

On these mountains, part of the grand
range of the Cordilleras, people are seized
with fainting, and a malady like sea-sick-
ness. The height above the level of the
sea is ten thousand feet.

Another disease often met with is blindness. The brilliance of the sun on the dazzling white of the snow has that effect; and the utmost caution is necessary to protect the eyes from the excessive glare.

Now and then the traveller is overtaken by a terrific storm of thunder and lightning. For hours the flashes continue with awful brilliancy, and the white snow looks as if tinged with blood.

The traveller is obliged to abandon his mule, and creep under the shelter of some rock or cave until the storm is over.

And here, too, in his journey over this wild part of the country, he comes upon those wonderful bridges that look like mere threads over an abyss.

The bridge is, in fact, merely a thick strip of hide or undressed leather that is fixed from one side of the torrent to the other.

A couple more strips are fixed over the chasm, and made to serve as a balustrade; and on this frail support the traveller has to venture his life, the bridge swaying with an unsteady motion at every step.

And more dangerous still is another bridge, made of a mere rope stretched from side to side, or bank to bank. A rough kind of chair is fastened to the rope, and in it the traveller seats himself, and is pulled slowly across by another rope attached to the chair, and in the hands of some one on the opposite bank.

The wild table-lands of Peru are called " the uninhabited." But Nature contrives a scanty kind of pasture. In some places are patches of the gentian, a true mountain-flower; and here is the verbena, and the ornament of our English gardens, the calceolaria. And here are a few dwarfed-looking shrubs that the inhabitants of this desolate region use for fuel, or to roof their miserable huts.

And here are some of the animals most valuable to man.   The beautiful little chinchilla has a relation here, with warm, soft fur that can be used as a garment. And here is the llama and the alpaca, and the tribe of creatures with shining wool that afford us a variety of materials for clothing.

And here is the mighty condor, the largest of the birds.   He soars to the highest peak of the Andes, and seems to look down on mountain, forest, and river. But, in reality, his piercing eye is searching for prey, and he will presently swoop on some poor mule that has fallen beneath its burden amid the bleak passes of the rocks.

Even here, wild as the scenery is, there are many beautiful birds.

Here is a species of Goose with snowy plumage and dark-green wings. And here, in the swamps and marshes, is the Scarlet Flamingo; and here is the Ibis, and the Plover, and the Gull.

In the sheltered valleys the traveller seems to step from the blasts of winter to the joys of perpetual spring. From the wretched hut of the Indian, on the heights yonder, he may, in a few hours, journey to the land of the Humming-Bird and the palm. Here he may feast on tropical fruits, and be surrounded by fields and meadows, rich in all the plenteousness of harvest.

The elevated country near Lima, the capital of Peru, is the home of the beautiful bird called the Cora Shear-Tail Humming-Bird. It is a tiny creature, and has two of its tail-feathers very long indeed.

Many of the Humming-Birds have been

named after precious stones ; such as the
emerald, the topaz, and the ruby, which
their flashing plumage resembles. The
bird just mentioned has given to it the
musical name of Cora—a name very common among the ladies of Peru.

Years ago, Peru was an independent
nation, and governed by the Incas, who
were priests as well as princes. The
Peruvians worshipped the Sun, and had
temples in his honour. And there were
maidens who were made priestesses of the
Sun, and were occupied in the idolatrous
rites of their religion, and in keeping alive
the fires and lamps upon the altars.

Cora is the name given to one of these
maidens by a French author in a story he
has written, and the scene of which is laid
in ancient Peru.

The Humming-Bird gets its title of
Cora from that story.

CHAPTER XVII.

THE GREEN-TAILED SYLPH.

IN the tropical world, everything appears to be on a grand scale. The forests, of which we have spoken, clothe an extent of country that seems almost boundless.

Great Britain itself would find ample space within the limits of one of these forests !

And equally vast are the far-stretching plains that occur in some parts of South America, and go by the name of " Llanos."

They reach for more than two hundred thousand miles ; and present a level sur-

face which, at certain seasons, is scorched
by the rays of the tropical sun.

This is the season when no rain falls,
and every living thing is scorched and
blasted by the intolerable heat.

But here and there grows a palm, that
is the blessing of the desert. While a
particle of moisture remains in the ground,
it collects round- the root of the tree, and
makes a little pool of water.

At one time of the year even these
pools are dried up.

The palm of which I am speaking is
called the Mauritia, or fan-palm, because
its leaves spread out in the shape of a fan.

A tribe of Indians who live in these
plains, subsist almost entirely on the produce of the fan-palm.

The meal-like substance contained in
the stem yields a nutritious article of
food, and is made into bread. The cone-

shaped fruit is also eaten, and the sap is made into a sweet wine.

At times, when the great river Orinoco overflows its banks, and inundates the dwellings of the Indians, they have recourse to the palm as to a place of refuge.

They climb nimbly up its branches with the agility of monkeys. Here they are often obliged to remain for some time; and they suspend their mats in the boughs, and take up their abode literally with the monkeys.

And a curious sight it is, to those on board some vessel sailing up the river, to behold the twinkling of lights in the tree-tops. The lights are kindled by the Indians in their aërial dwellings.

Another palm grows in the territory of New Granada, that is of equal service to man.

Its leaves are very large, and are used

to thatch the native huts. But it is the nut that yields the substance to which I refer.

It yields a clear tasteless juice, that is refreshing as a beverage in that hot climate ; but if it is allowed to remain untouched, it soon becomes white and milky, and in the end sets hard and solid, like ivory.

This is the vegetable ivory of which so many toys and fancy articles are made. If the vegetable ivory is put in water it will soften ; but on being taken out, it quickly becomes hard again. It is so like the ivory of the elephant's tusks, that it cannot be distinguished from it.

A beautiful bird lives in this part of the world, and frequents the banks of the great rivers.

It belongs to the tribe of Humming-Birds that have tails more or less forked.

The name of Sylph has been given to it, perhaps on account of its exceeding grace and loveliness. The colours of its sapphire throat, and emerald crown, and olive-green feathers, blend harmoniously together. Its long, forked, green tail is tipped with yellow.

To this family group belong many birds with tails deeply forked, and that are of great beauty. There is the Racket-tailed Humming-Bird, that has a spoon-like tip at the end of each fork, a little like the Racket-tailed Kingfisher; and the Black-capped Humming-Bird, with a black crest, and tail-feathers also black, and length-ened to a considerable extent; and the Swallow-tailed Humming-Bird, with a tail of indigo-blue.

CHAPTER XVIII.

THIS bird, though it comes last in the volume, is by no means least in beauty.

It is one of the loveliest of birds.

The shape of its body very much resembles that of the Humming-Bird Hawk-Moth, of which we have spoken before.

Its wings are small, and of a purplish-brown colour. The neck and upper part of the body are clothed with green and gold, and the feathers are arranged to look like a gorget. The tail is chestnut-red,

7

and is slightly forked.   But the most brilliant ornament worn by the Coquette— for such it is—consists of a splendid orange crest of a shining red, and the feathers of which rise up into a point.   Nothing can exceed the beauty of this sparkling crest, as it glitters in the sun.   It gives to the bird an appearance that can hardly be described.

The Coquette has even been spoken of as a " winged flame."

The home of the Coquette is in the country of Bolivia, and along the banks of the great rivers.

For the rivers in America, like the mountains and the plains, are on a scale of the utmost magnitude.   They wind along with the grandeur almost of the ocean.

The giant river of South America is the Amazon, that in places spreads out into an expanse of water of a pale yellowish orange, and is as much as six miles in breadth.

Trunks of trees, and fruit and leaves, and fragments of the forest, float in vast quantities down the river. And beds of aquatic plants line the shore. Masses of these plants, looking like sea-weeds, detach themselves, here and there, and form floating islands.

On either bank of the river is the dense and mighty forest, that presents us with a succession of pictures. Here are stems of different colours,—black, red, yellow, and silvery gray. And here is the feathery palm ; and here are festoons and garlands of colour, as the parasitic plants droop from the branches and, in places, touch the water.

The water's edge is alive with birds. Here are crowds of water-fowl. Here is the Heron, standing patiently for hours, his eye fixed on the water beneath, in which he hopes presently to spy out a fish. And here is the Scarlet Flamingo, like a soldier sentinel, and the White Ibis, and many more.

Overhead fly the sea-birds, the Gull and the Tern, as though this mighty river were the ocean. The Gulls utter all night their hoarse cry. By day they often amuse themselves by sitting in a row on some floating log of wood in the middle of the stream, and sailing down, as if they enjoyed the voyage.

They deposit their eggs in the sand-banks. And the Indian, who is very observant of the habits of the birds, says that in the middle of the day they carry drops of water in their bills, to moisten the eggs, and prevent them from being spoiled by the excessive heat.

And here, as in the sea, a shoal of porpoises will tumble clumsily about. And, to the terror of those who are sailing on the water, a grim alligator will swim slowly by.

The waters abound in fish. And here is found a species of salmon, called the " piranga." This little creature bites terribly, and attacks everything it meets with. The waters will be stained with the blood of its victim.

A person who chances to bathe or swim in the neighbourhood of the pirangas is sure to suffer. He will be lacerated by a number of sharp teeth, that seem as if they were bent upon devouring him.

The poor stag is now and then actually devoured. When pressed by an enemy, he will plunge into the water, and attempt to swim across ; but he will be so bitten and wounded by the merciless pirangas, that he sinks from exhaustion, and becomes their prey.

The river forms a line of division between one tribe of creatures and another.

The monkeys that live in the forest on one side of the river differ from the monkeys on the other side. Thus the river is like a sea that divides territories and races one from the other.

Here are two separate regions teeming with different occupants. And, as if still further to keep up the resemblance to the ocean, the hoarse cry of the Petrel and the Sea-mew is heard; and they dart along the water and skim the waves, as though they mistook them for the briny deep!

·FINIS·

www.ingramcontent.com/pod-product-compliance
Lightning Source LLC
Chambersburg PA
CBHW040512290326
41930CB00035B/1

* 9 7 8 1 5 8 2 1 8 8 4 5 4 *

Breaking Free from Pain and Opioids
Discovering the Hypnosis Option

Roberta Fernandez, BCH, CPHI
Board Certified Hypnotist
Certified Professional Hypnosis Instructor

Copyright © 2016 Roberta K. Fernandez
All rights reserved.

ISBN: 0692745866
ISBN 13: 9780692745861